Reflections

Reflections

By Tiffany J. Breed

A book of photographs featuring reflections.

ISBN: 1502583860
ISBN-13: 978-1502583864

Books by

Tiffany J. Breed

The Love Of A Child

Baseball Game

Poems By Tiffany

Reflections

www.ingramcontent.com/pod-product-compliance
Lightning Source LLC
Chambersburg PA
CBHW050857290526
45792CB00002B/635
* 9 7 8 1 5 0 2 5 8 3 8 6 4 *